WISDOM
FOR KINGDOM LIVING

Wisdom for Kingdom Living

FIRST EDITION
Published in February 2024

Y.A.M. MEDIA
YANNI AYANA MEDIA, LLC
www.YanniAyana.com

ISBN: 979-8-9864151-7-8

Library of Congress Registration
Ayana, Yanni
The Inheritance: Heirs Restored
Registration Number: TXu 2-397-818 | Oct 08, 2023

Category: Christian Living

Library of Congress Cataloging-in-Publication Data

Author: Yanni Ayana Media, LLC |
YAM.Books@outlook.com

Cover Design and Layout: Eli Blyden Sr. |
www.EliTheBookGuy.com

Printed in the United States of America by: A&A
Printing & Publishing | www.PrintShopCentral.com

ACKNOWLEDGEMENTS

I thank you GOD for giving me the grace, ability, and courage to author books about the message of the kingdom of God in the earth.

I would also like to thank my mother Maria Morrison, for her love, time, encouragement, and support in all my endeavors!

Thank you to my father Michael Bernard, my wonderful sister Dr. Alicia Francois, Uncle Trevor, Tina, and Pastors Daniel and Sabrina Mangrum for their love for me through the years.

A special thank you to my Pastors Gary and Patricia Newton for their love, support, and for faithfully teaching me the message of the kingdom of God in every sermon.

I would also like to thank my loving family, leaders, and friends.

Thank you everyone for your support, and prayers! It means more to me than you will ever know.

God richly bless you!
–Yanni Ayana

CONTENTS

WISDOM
FOR KINGDOM LIVING

Written by: YANNI AYANA

INTRODUCTION

"Wisdom for Kingdom Living," is a short, and simple book that is purposed to provide understanding about the message of the kingdom of God that Jesus preached throughout His ministry on earth. I hope that it will give you a better understanding about the importance of knowing your identity as a child of God, the power available to you through your faith, and insight on how to become more stable in your relationship with God and others. It is my prayer that you will receive wisdom and apply these kingdom lessons to improve your overall quality of life.

Living a kingdom lifestyle requires a new mindset, willingness to believe, obey, and agree with Jesus's teachings.

As you begin to understand His Word, your faith will grow, and you will be able to experience God's love and promises shared in His Word as His beloved child.

Jesus preached the gospel of the kingdom of God. We are to follow His example, and teachings within our own lives. May the knowledge shared in this book, bring revelation and transformation as you submit your will to God and experience the benefits of living a kingdom life!

You are important in God's plan of redemption. He desires to reposition you in your rightful place as His beloved child and expand His kingdom on the earth through a loving relationship with you!

God bless you and thank you for reading this book!

— Yanni Ayana

INFLUENCE

*"Don't adapt to the energy in
the room. Influence the energy in
the room."*
— Unknown

When God created you, He designed you and made you with a purpose. Through your relationship with Him, you will discover who you are, and how to use your gifts.

In a relationship with the Lord, communication and love go both ways. When your relationship with God is strong, His influence grows greater in your life. God's influence has transformative effects! His love touches every area of your being. God's love and His word can transform your character, personality, and behavior through your faith and love for Him.

God must be the highest priority in your life. It is important to desire His Will, above your own. Obedience to His Word will help you stay in right standing in your relationship with Him. Your love relationship with the Lord will not only transform you but touch every person in your life.

God has placed people in your life because you have something to offer! You are unique! You have something to give. You have purpose and you are powerful! God's presence in your life, makes you impactful and gives you tremendous influence everywhere you go. God and You are a team. He wants to share His love for others through the gifts, talents, and personality He has bestowed upon you. His purpose is to first transform you with His Word, then use this knowledge to expand His kingdom, through your Light.

YOU ARE THE ANSWER

Everything God makes has a purpose! When God made you, He designed you to fulfill a need. You are the answer to a problem! Your personality, interests, gifts, and the topics that you are enthusiastic about, are clues to the plan God has designed for you.

God is omnipotent (all-knowing) It is important to remember that through Christ Jesus, you are sons and daughters of God! You have the Holy Spirit within you! So, anytime you are confronted with a challenge, be still, and listen to His voice! He will speak to you and endow you with wisdom.

Proverbs 3:5-6 (KJV) *"Trust in the LORD with all thine heart; and lean not unto thine own understanding. ⁶ In all thy ways acknowledge him, and he shall direct thy paths."*

So, whenever you are confronted with a problem, believe that God is your Deliverer! Use your faith in Christ Jesus, to pray and receive answers and direction! God wants to expand your influence in your environment for His kingdom! He desires for you to walk in His favor and counsel in every area of your life. Depend on God. Rely on Him! He wants to help you! He wants to give you the solutions, to help you navigate victoriously through this life. Jesus said to ask Him for what you need!

Matthew 7:7-8 (KJV), *"Ask, and it shall be given..."*

James 4:2 (KJV), *"... ye have not, because ye ask not."*

God has made you capable and competent! Do not bow to fear, anxiety, and the negative words that come to attack your confidence! Have faith in God!

God has placed you in your environment for a reason. You are on assignment for Him. He wants to bring answers through you, as you rely on Him. Remember anytime you are faced with a problem that you are the answer, and an overcomer!

USE WISDOM

James 1:5 (KJV*)*, *"If any of you lack wisdom, let him ask of God, that giveth to all men liberally, and upbraideth not; and it shall be given him."*

Proverbs 15:33 (KJV), *"The fear of the Lord is the instruction of wisdom: and before honor is humility.*

Spiritual wisdom helps you discern a matter. It gives you the ability to judge and assess a situation and know what the best course of action is at that time. Wisdom does not make you cocky, because it requires humility and submission to God, to receive it!

When God's wisdom is manifested, it increases your influence in everything you do! You will obtain winning results and be a blessing to everyone connected to you. Wisdom helps you recognize the importance of timing, and how to apply emotional intelligence to relationships.

The Bible shares that there is kingdom wisdom and carnal wisdom. Carnal wisdom will reap toxic traits of jealousy, selfishness, and conflicts with others.

> James 4:13-17 (KJV), *"Who is a wise man and endued with knowledge among you? Let him shew out of a good conversation his works with meekness of wisdom.*
> *But if ye have bitter envying and strife in your hearts, glory not, and lie not against the truth. This wisdom descendeth not from above, but is earthly, sensual, devilish.*

*For where envying and strife is,
there is confusion and every evil
work.
But the wisdom that is from above
is first pure, then peaceable,
gentle, and easy to be intreated,
full of mercy and good fruits,
without partiality, and without
hypocrisy."*

All relationships are important to God. He designed you to need Him as your Source. Receive His love, and then share it with others.

Proverbs 11:30 (KJV), *"The fruit
of the righteous is a tree of life;
and he that winneth souls is wise."*

God wants to expand His kingdom, reach more of His children with His love through you! He knows that relationships with others can be incredibly challenging in our daily lives. No one is perfect!

Every relationship requires forgiveness. Forgiveness is necessary for both people involved to heal and grow. Only God can help you walk in love towards others! Ask God for wisdom today and receive it by faith.

BE MINDFUL

What information are you feeding your mind on a regular basis? Know that whatever input you receive, whether verbal or visual, molds your values, personality, and belief system.

Information is received through watching and listening. The content you take in repeatedly gets lodged into your subconscious mind, and will be displayed in your habits, values, beliefs, and behavior. The subconscious mind has embedded information that has been accumulated and stored over extended periods of time. Your mind retains beliefs about yourself, God, relationships, and devises conclusions about life based on your experiences.

God desires for you to renew your subconscious mind.

> Romans 12:2 (KJV), *"And be not conformed to this world: but be ye transformed by the renewing of your mind, that ye may prove what is that good, and acceptable, and perfect, will of God."*

For you to fulfill your purpose in Him, you will need to replace the old information, with His Word, morals, and values. When you decide to change your mind and fill it with the Word of God, your intimacy with God will develop. Prayer, Bible teachings, and worship will help you make more decisions and choices that will agree with His Word. You will learn to obey the promptings of the Holy Spirit within you.

The more you agree with God's Word, your subconscious mind will be able to discern ideas, and thoughts that are contrary. You will make more decisions to submit to God's Word, and this will manifest changes in your behavior, emotions, and character. It is important to be conscious of the types of information you allow into your mind.

GOD SEES ME!

*"And she called the name of the
Lord that spake unto her,
Thou God seest me:"*
– Genesis 16:13 (KJV)

Life is so busy! It is easy to feel alone and invisible. So many people suffer silently, because they have no one to share their thoughts and feelings with. It seems as if no one cares or will understand them. Whenever you feel alone remember EL ROI- The God who sees! God sees you and cares about everything that concerns you. He knows where you hurt. He sees your silent tears and hears your internal screams of frustration.

He knows the times where you feel devalued and insignificant. He will heal you and comfort you.

John 14:18 (KJV), *"I will not leave you comfortless: I will come to you."*

2 Corinthians 1:4 (KJV), *"(God) Who comforteth us in all our tribulation, that we may be able to comfort them which are in any trouble, by the comfort wherewith we ourselves are comforted of God."*

When your heart is overwhelmed, remember you have God's undivided attention! You are His child, His beloved! Humble yourself, go to God in prayer, share with Him, and receive His comfort.

GOD SEES YOU! EL ROI- the GOD Who Sees Me

STRENGTH

L ife is full of ups and downs; each day is unknown. You never know what will happen: a phone call, text, or event can change your life forever. You need strength to endure difficult challenges or transitions, in moments when you are weak, full of grief, and unsure about what to do. Go to God and ask for strength.

> Psalms 46:1 (NIV), *"God is our refuge and strength, an ever-present help in trouble."*

When there are tasks that you dread, trust God to help you.

Isaiah 41:10 (KJV), "*Fear thou not; for I am with thee: be not dismayed; for I am thy God: I will strengthen thee; yea, I will help thee; yea, I will uphold thee with the Right hand of my righteousness.*"

The Lord God is your peace! He will cover you in His peace when you focus and trust in Him.

John 14:27 (NIV), "*Peace I leave with you; my peace I give you. I do not give to you as the world gives. Do not let your hearts be troubled and do not be afraid.*"

If you struggle with trust and abandonment issues, please believe, and know that the Lord will not forsake you! The Lord will not fail you!

Hebrews 13:5 (AMPC), *"...for He [God] [b]Himself has said, I will not in any way fail you nor [c]give you up nor leave you without support. [I will] not, [d][I will] not, [I will] not in any degree leave you helpless nor forsake nor [e]let [you] down ([f]relax My hold on you)! [[g]Assuredly not!]"*

In your relationship with the Lord, remember He is with you and will not abandon you. He is your Source and ability. Through your faith in Jesus Christ His Son, you have a covenant with your Heavenly Father, and He is committed to you! You can trust God with your life!

Life will have its challenges and uncertainties, but you do not have to be strong on your own. Go to God, He will give you His strength!

TALK TO ME

There is a song by Anita Baker that I love! It is called "Talk to Me!" In the song she is pleading with someone to share their heart with her. She asks them to share what is bothering them, to not keep the matter locked within themselves. She pleads for them to be open and share, so healing can begin in their relationship.

When I hear this song, it reminds me of God's heart towards His children. He wants you to talk to Him! He yearns for you to share your joys, concerns, and life experiences with Him daily! God wants a dialogue with you! The Lord wants a loving open, honest, candid relationship with you.

God wants to heal you where you are hurt and broken. He wants to free you from the torture of anxiety in your life which is rooted in fear.

> 1 John 4:18 (KJV), *"There is no fear in love; but perfect love casteth out fear: because fear hath torment."*

Trust God, remove the doubt, and He will allow your soul to rest in His peace.

Don't live an isolated, independent life, when you can have a fulfilling relationship with the LORD. When you received salvation through faith in Jesus Christ, the Holy Spirit came to live inside of you! The Holy Spirit is the Spirit of the Father living in you to help you realize your divine purpose in this life. God wants to help you! You do not have to be independent and solve your own problems or fix your own issues.

Matthew 6:31-33 (KJV),
"Therefore take no thought,
saying, What shall we eat? or,
What shall we drink? or,
Wherewithal shall we be clothed?
(For after all these things do the
Gentiles seek:) for your heavenly
Father knoweth that ye have need
of all these things.
But seek ye first the kingdom of
God, and his righteousness; and
all these things shall be added
unto you."

Matthew 11:28 (NIV) Jesus says,
"Come to me, all you who are
weary and burdened, and I will
give you rest."

Whenever something is wrong, or when things are going well in your life, do not leave God out! Share your heart with Him! Be available for Him! Remember Him throughout your day. Remember Him when you are relaxed! Remember Him when you are overwhelmed. God shares with you in your thoughts, suggestions, and through other people. He wants you to lean on and depend on Him in every area of your life! He is the only One that can help you navigate through your life with Victory! God says to you, "Please, *Talk to ME!*"

LOVE

"A new commandment I give unto you, That ye love one another; as I have loved you, that ye also love one another. By this shall all men know that ye are my disciples, if ye have love one to another."
— John 13:34-35 (KJV)

Love is the culture of the kingdom of God. God is Love. It is His nature, and should be our nature as well, when we walk as one in Him. Love is the attribute that sets you apart as children of God and is a common need in the hearts of all people.

John 13:35 (NIV), *"By this everyone will know that you are my disciples, if you love one another."*

God loves you with an unconditional love! Knowledge of your identity in Him as His beloved child will build your self-esteem. When you begin to agree with Him by faith about who you are in Him, then you will grow to love and accept yourself as His son or daughter.

Jesus stated in Matthew 22:37-39 (NIV), what is the first and greatest commandment:

> *"Thou shalt love the Lord thy God*
> *with all thy heart, and with all thy*
> *soul, and with all thy mind. This is*
> *the first and great commandment.*
> *And the second is like unto it,*
> *Thou shalt love thy neighbor*
> *as thyself."*

The ability to love others as God loves us, is the ultimate demonstration of your new nature in Christ Jesus. Loving others, and forgiving offenses can be very difficult! People are not always easy to love. They are not always lovable, kind, or respectful! It is only because of our desire to please the Lord and do His Will that we humble ourselves before Him, and ask Him for help to obey this great commandment!

God knows that we are not able to love others with a pure heart without His guidance. He gave us a checklist in 1Corinthians 13:1-7, which teaches us how love behaves and what it looks like in our relationship with others. It is a great measuring tool for us to examine our love walk in every relationship in our lives. We need the power of God to love Him with all our hearts, minds, and strength (which will help us to obey Him), and practice loving others genuinely.

Walking in love does not mean that you are gullible, naïve, or support others by being an enabler. It is a miserable existence when you are a people-pleaser! God does not want us to be controlled, used, or deceived! You do not have to get caught up with toxic relationships, and manipulative traps! When you submit your life to God, He will give you wisdom, and help you establish healthy boundaries that may upset others. You will have to maintain a strong stance and guard your heart amid rejection from others. Staying consistent through the drama and offense will make you stronger! It will help you become more stable in your emotions.

God will reward your obedience, as you take courage to develop healthy non-toxic relationships in your life. He will bless you with divine connections through people chosen to be a blessing in your life, and vice versa. There is an encouraging quote that says,

"God will always give you the BEST, when you leave the choices up to HIM!"

You are God's representative of love. If you rely on Him to help you, He will give you the power to treat all people with respect. You do not have to push your faith, values, and ideas on people! Just live what you believe! Live your life to please God and obey the leading of the Holy Spirit! Keep your heart pure before God! He will strengthen you so that you can walk in love with wisdom.

> 1 John 4:20-21 (KJV), *"If a man say, I love God, and hateth his brother, he is a liar: for he that loveth not his brother whom he hath seen, how can he love God whom he hath not seen?*

> [21] *And this commandment have we from him, That he who loveth God love his brother also."*

People will always observe you, to decide within themselves if your love is authentic! They will come to their own conclusion on whether they want to connect with the Light within you. In the meantime, continue to manifest LOVE.

SURRENDER

*"You are not a drop in the ocean.
You are the entire ocean,
in a drop."*

– Rumi

I love this quote by the poet Rumi because it is a great reminder that everything about God abides on the inside of you!

In your relationship with God, it is easy to spend a lot of time lamenting over your short-comings, flaws, and mistakes, that you made on your life journey. When you focus on these things, there is an inner subconscious belief that you will not become all that He desires you to be. It is important to know that everything God has created you to become is already inside of you. He is committed to helping you in your transformation back to His original design and purpose. He will complete the work He has started inside of you.

> Philippians 1:6 (KJV) says,
> *"Being confident of this very thing, that He who has begun a good work in you will perform it until the day of Jesus Christ:"*

You are made in the image and likeness of God. You are His child, and offspring on the earth. Through submission to His guidance, you will have the ability to have self-control (temperance) and walk in dominion and authority in every area of your life. The key to kingdom living and manifestation is dependency on God! You must practice being always dependent on Him, for your needs and direction. God is the greater power within you. Your humility will allow His power, influence, and wisdom to flow through you.

> 1 John 4:4 (KJV), *"Ye are of God, little children, ... greater is He that is in you, than he that is in the world."*

You are chosen by God to share His nature, culture, and lifestyle in the earth. You have within you His wisdom, knowledge, and understanding through faith in His Son Jesus Christ. God wants to help you accomplish His will in your life.

> In John 15:16 (NIV) Jesus said, *"You did not choose me, but I chose you and appointed you so that you might go and bear fruit- fruit that will last- and so that whatever you ask in my name the Father will give you."*

Anytime you feel like you are unworthy, incapable, incompetent; re-member God lives in you! You are not trying to be the ocean or trying to be great. You are the entire ocean in a drop! You contain within you God Himself, and all His greatness, and power!

As an isolated, separated drop of ocean water- you are limited. However, when the drop of ocean water releases its independence, surrender, and becomes ONE with the ocean - nothing is im-possible to accomplish! As the drop reconnects with the ocean, it can no longer be found as a drop alone. It no longer has an individual identity! It is consumed by the ocean and flows in unison with it.

Nurture and build your relationship with the Lord. Communicate, prioritize your intimate time with Him. Know that Christ lives with in you, and you have access to all that He is! Christ is everything you need! You no longer have to be self-conscious as an isolated drop! Release yourself into the ocean- which is God's presence, and you will become more God-conscious. There are no limits in God, and when you are One with Him there are no limits within you. Jesus prayed in John 17:21 (KJV),

> *21 "That they all may be one; as thou, Father art in me, and I in thee, that they also may be ONE in US: that the world may believe that thou hast sent me."*

You are sons, daughters of the royal family of God through your faith in Jesus Christ. Believe and agree with who God says you are! Surrender the idea of changing yourself and relying on your own abilities. Surrender your life to God and depend on Him in every area of your life. Allow the Lord's Will to be accomplished in your daily life! Be mindful, that He is always with you and desires to flow through you!

Become ONE with God and no
longer live independently.

Become "One with the ocean and
no longer a drop."

SURRENDER yourself and fall in
love with the Lord!

RIGHTEOUS NATURE

Romans 5:19 (KJV) *"For as by one man's disobedience many were made sinners, so by the obedience of ONE shall many be made **righteous**."*

Romans 14:17 (KJV) *"For the kingdom of God is not meat and drink; but **righteousness**, and peace, and joy in the Holy Ghost."*

Nature: "the innate or essential qualities of a person." Did you know that when you receive Jesus Christ as your Lord and Savior you also receive His righteous nature?

When Adam sinned in the garden of Eden, all mankind automatically received a sinful nature because he was no longer submitted under the Spirit of God. When

Jesus died on the cross, He paid for all sins past, present, and future with His holy blood. In His resurrection, He gave all mankind His righteous nature automatically.

> Romans 5:19 (KJV) *"For as by one man's disobedience many were made sinners, so by the obedience of one shall many be made righteous."*

All who receive Jesus Christ as their Lord and Savior are now submitted unto God and receives His gift of righteousness. Righteousness is being in right standing with God. Christ's righteousness empowers us to walk in the dominion and authority God originally intended for us in every area of our lives.

Genesis 1:26 (KJV), *"And God said, Let us make man in our image, after our likeness; and let them have dominion over the fish of the sea, and over the fowl of the air, and over the cattle, and over all the earth and over every creeping thing that creepeth upon the earth."*

Luke 10:19 (KJV) Jesus shared, *"Behold, I give unto you power to tread on serpents and scorpions, and over all the power of the enemy: and nothing shall by any means hurt you."*

When you make mistakes, get restored quickly to right standing with God. Use your faith to believe in the scripture,

1 John 1:9 (KJV), *"If we confess our sins, He (Christ Jesus) is faithful and just to forgive our*

sins, and to cleanse us from all unrighteousness."

Romans 8:1 (AMPC), *"Therefore, [there is] now no condemnation (no adjudging guilty of wrong) for those who are in Christ Jesus, who live [and] walk not after the dictates of the flesh, but after the dictates of the Spirit."*

Confess your sins to God in prayer and repent for the wrong actions. Repentance means to change your mind about the sin and agree with God on His stance on the matter. God will then help you overcome your old mindset and behaviors. Before you know it, you will witness your own victory over old habits and behaviors. You will manifest your righteous nature, your right position in Christ, and walk in victory in every area of your life!

2 Corinthians 5:17 (KJV)
"Therefore if any man be in Christ, he is a new creature: old things are passed away; behold, all things are become new."

2 Corinthians 5:21 (AMP)
"He (God) made Christ who knew no sin to [judicially] be sin on our behalf, so that in Him we would become the righteousness of God [that is, we would be made acceptable to Him and placed in a right relationship with Him by His gracious lovingkindness]."

No longer cower in shame over past or recent failures! Remember to repent, get up, and put on Christ righteousness by faith! Enjoy your relationship with the Lord!

KINGDOM AMBASSADOR

Ambassador: "An accredited diplomat sent by a country as its official representative to a foreign country."

> 2 Corinthians 5:20 (NIV), *"We are therefore Christ's ambassadors, as though God were making his appeal through us. We implore you on Christ's behalf: Be reconciled to God."*

Ambassadors are diplomatic agents selected by the king or an official of their government. They must represent their government's culture, lifestyle, and nature of the king, in another territory or country. As an ambassador of the kingdom of Heaven, you are to influence the people in your environment by being a living example of the moral standards, and beliefs of God's kingdom.

Heaven is the name of God's kingdom. God is a sovereign King. God wants His children to have dominion and authority in the earth. Earth is a colony of the kingdom of Heaven. A kingdom is a government. He wants His kingdom to be established on earth, through a loving relationship with His children.

Jesus came to reconcile us back to God and His kingdom. The scriptures in the book of Isaiah and Matthew announces the coming and purpose of Jesus.

> Isaiah 9:6 (NIV), *"For to us a child is born,
> to us a son is given, and the government will be on his shoulders."*

Matthew 4:17 (KJV), *"From that time Jesus began to preach, and to say, Repent: for the kingdom of heaven is at hand."*

In Luke 4:43 (NIV), Jesus stated his purpose and intent.
"But he (Jesus) said, "I must proclaim the good news of the kingdom of God to the other towns also, because that is why I was sent."

Earth is a colony of the kingdom of Heaven. God wants His children to have dominion and authority in the earth, as He governs His kingdom in heaven. He wants His kingdom to be established on earth, through a loving relationship with you.

As chosen diplomats of God's kingdom, we are to prioritize our relationship with the Lord. By reading the Bible and obeying His Word- you will fulfill your divine purpose. God wants to express His love for others through His relationship with you.

When you keep God first, He will be with you, and take care of you! There is no lack in His kingdom.

Matthew 6:31-33 (KJV),
*"Therefore take no thought,
saying, What shall we eat? Or,
What shall we drink? Or,
Wherewithal shall we be clothed?
(For after all these things do the
Gentiles seek; for your heavenly
Father knoweth that ye have need
of all these things.
But seek ye first the kingdom of
God, and his righteousness; and
all these things shall be added
unto you."*

God has chosen you. Your life has a purpose! As representatives of our King and heavenly Father, you are to agree with His Word as the final authority and governing power over every area of your life. God has equipped you with gifts, talents, and everything you need for the assignment appointed to you here on earth. Always remember that you are Christ's Kingdom Ambassadors.

KINGDOM CITIZENSHIP

Ephesians 2:18-20 (NIV), *"For through him (Jesus Christ) we both have access to the Father by one Spirit. Consequently, you are no longer foreigners and strangers, but fellow **citizens** with God's people and also members of his household."*

Every day in the news media, you hear of people migrating to richer countries in hopes of experiencing a better quality of life. However, to receive the rights and benefits of that country, its government must approve of their residency, and if applicable, may provide opportunity for citizenship.

"Citizenship: relationship between an individual and a state to which the individual owes allegiance and in turn is entitled to its protection. Citizenship is the most privileged form of nationality. It provides other privileges, particularly protection abroad. Citizenship implies the status of freedom with accompanying responsibilities."

– Britannica.com

The scripture Ephesians 2:19 (NIV), explains that we are citizens of the kingdom of Heaven, and family members of the household of God. We are sons and daughters of God through our faith in Jesus Christ, and through our intentional obedience to the Holy Spirit.

Romans 8:14 (NIV), *"For those who are led by the Spirit of God are the children of God."*

All citizens are to adhere to the laws of their government. The Word of God (Holy Bible) is the constitution of the kingdom of God. You must study it to know God's intentions and expectations. When Christ fulfilled the law, He gave you His righteousness, the Holy Spirit, and access to the rights, and benefits of the kingdom of Heaven. God wants you to have rulership. Your rights as citizens gives you the authority to do His will in the earth through Jesus Christ.

You can also give up your rights and benefits through disobedience or igno-rance of the Word. To reap the reward of citizenship, you must know your rights! If you are unaware of what belongs to you as a child of God, and a citizen of His kingdom, you will always live below the standards bequeathed to you. This is why the enemy wants you to live in ignorance, by not reading, understanding the Word of God, and through receiving erroneous teachings.

> Hosea 4:6 (KJV), *"My people are destroyed for lack of knowledge…"*

> Proverbs 4:7 (KJV), *"… with all thy getting get understanding."*

Community

The rights and privileges of citizenship are not for you to become selfish or isolated. In the kingdom of God, there is commonwealth, and all citizens are to have a mindset of love and community by caring about others. In the kingdom of God, the greatest commandment is to love God, yourself, and others.

Matthew 22:36-40 (KJV),
"Master, which is the great
commandment in the law?
Jesus said unto him, Thou shalt
love the Lord thy God with all thy
heart, and with all thy soul, and
with all thy mind.
This is the first and great
commandment.
And the second is like unto it,
Thou shalt love thy neighbour
as thyself.
On these two commandments hang
all the law and the prophets."

It is your love for God that will motivate you to obey His Word, even when others are not in agreement with you. An intimate relationship with the Lord will open your heart to love others as you love yourself. The more you recognize His great love for you, it will become easier to love other people.

We are not to live independently of Him, but to depend on the King for all our needs. As it is stated in Ephesians 2:19 (NIV), we are of the "household" of God. The kingdom of God operates as a community. As believers in Christ Jesus, you have a common union with others as brethren, and God as our heavenly Father.

As citizens, and children of God, we must keep Him first, and obey His leading in every area of our lives. Obedience will enable you to experience the fullness of God's protection, rights, benefits, and grace. When we keep God first, and remain in continual fellowship with Him, all that belongs to you in the kingdom of God, will be manifested in your daily life.

Receive

If you have not received Jesus Christ as your Lord and Savior, you can give your life to Him today with a simple prayer of faith.

Romans 10:9-10 (KJV), *"That if thou shalt confess with thy mouth the Lord Jesus, and shalt believe in thine heart that God hath raised him from the dead, thou shalt be saved."*

The work of the believer is not to be consumed with busy works for God. It is more important to seek Him for direction, obey Him, and have faith in His Son Jesus Christ.

John 6:29 (KJV), *"Jesus answered and said unto them, This is the work of God, that ye believe on him whom he hath sent."*

Romans 10:10-13 (KJV) continues, *"For with the heart man believeth unto righteousness; and with the mouth confession is made unto salvation.*

For the scripture saith, Whosoever believeth on him shall not be ashamed.

For there is no difference between the Jew and the Greek: for the same Lord over all is rich unto all that call upon him.

For whosoever shall call upon the name of the Lord shall be saved."

When you receive Jesus Christ as your Lord and Savior, pray to receive the gifts of the Holy Spirit of God into your heart. He will help lead and guide you into all Truth. The Holy Spirit will give you access to God our Father through your faith in His Son Jesus Christ. Rejoice! The All-powerful King has chosen you to be a part of His perfect kingdom.

God will be faithful to you all your days, as you set your mind to be obedient and faithful to Him. Get your citizenship to the only perfect government that exists! In this kingdom, the Most High God is your heavenly Father and King! Renew your mind, and use your faith, to receive your rights, protection, and government assistance from the kingdom of God today!

KINGDOM CITIZENSHIP

"It is important to love others. In the kingdom of God, you have to think about the community! You have to care about other people!"
– Christine Bland-Millard

REFERENCES

- Holy Bible
- www.BibleGateway.com
- www.Google.com
- www.Britannica.com

OTHER BOOKS BY
YANNI AYANA

Y.A.M. MEDIA

Yanni Ayana Media, LLC
www.YanniAyana.com

o Do you have a yearning for wisdom and inspiration?

o Do you want to learn how to apply God's Word in your daily life?

o Do you want to know how to handle daily challenges?

Then this book,
Wisdom *for* Everyday Living
is for you!

God wants you to enjoy your life in Him. Your relationship with God is not purposed to be burdensome. "Wisdom For Everyday Living," is designed to help you think, live, and learn how to apply biblical wisdom in your daily walk with God.

When betrayed by someone you love- do you forgive the offense to give them another chance?

* * *

King Sequoia, Coast, and Don of the eternal tree kingdom Arbol- are forced to confront the diabolical plans of an influential leader named, Jaccard.

Jaccard's jealousy of King Sequoia's power and authority led to sedition.
Denounced Jaccard, now called KUDZU aims his revenge at what is most dear to King Sequoia's heart.

* * *

What is the depth of King Sequoia's love for the unfaithful?

Will KUDZU's plan for revenge give him the power and control he always wanted?

LOVE knows NO LIMITS.

Cuando te traiciona alguien a quien amas,
¿perdonas la ofensa para darle otra
oportunidad?

* * *

El rey Sequoia, Coast y Don del reino de
los árboles eternos, Arbol, se ven obligados
a enfrentarse a los diabólicos planes de un
influyente líder llamado, Jaccard.

Los celos de Jaccard por el poder y la
autoridad del Rey Sequoia han llevado a
la sedición.

El denunciado Jaccard, ahora llamado
KUDZU apunta su venganza a lo más
querido por el corazón del Rey Sequoia.

* * *

¿Cuál es la profundidad del amor del rey
Sequoia por los infieles?

¿El plan de venganza de KUDZU le dará
el poder y el control que siempre quiso?

El AMOR no tiene LÍMITES.

ABOUT THE AUTHOR

Yanni Ayana is the president of Yanni Ayana Media, LLC (Y.A.M.)

She is also an author, and bible teacher with a radio ministry broadcast that continues to bless people around the world. The objective of her media ministry is to teach the message of the kingdom of God with simplicity and understanding.

Yanni's love for bible stories, and storytelling is vividly expressed in her writings and bible teaching ministry. Her heart's desire is for others to have a loving relationship with God, through their faith in His Son Jesus Christ. She believes this relationship is vital, for God to fulfill his original plan and design for our lives.

www.ingramcontent.com/pod-product-compliance
Lightning Source LLC
Chambersburg PA
CBHW060348130626
46553CB00003B/1136